FAIRGROUND LORRIES

CARL JOHNSON

AMBERLEY

First published 2024

Amberley Publishing
The Hill, Stroud
Gloucestershire, GL5 4EP

www.amberley-books.com

ISBN 978 1 3981 0084 8 (print)
ISBN 978 1 3981 0085 5 (ebook)

British Library Cataloguing in Publication Data.
A catalogue record for this book is available from the British Library.

Origination by Amberley Publishing.
Printed in the UK.

Introduction

Having worked (and occasionally still do) on the fairs, and with my interest in lorries, it became second nature to photograph the vehicles that could be seen on the 'tobers' (fairgrounds). Whenever the opportunity to spot fair lorries arose, the camera was given an airing.

Being a part time 'gaff lad' I can honestly say that the fairground is not all bright lights, pretty girls and candy floss! In fact, it can be hard work, and sometimes not always in the best conditions. If you are building up or pulling down and there is a downpour, the show must go on. Being cold, wet and miserable was all part of the game. Worse still, some of the 'back end' runs can often be a victim of the cold, with snow and hard frosts not being unknown. Trying to wrestle with tarpaulins that are brittle with frost is no joke, and with the ride components made of steel, etc., well, you can imagine. I remember a number of years back, when it was fashionable to have a moustache, pulling down after a bonfire 'do' at Donington, near Telford, and having a good layer of frost on mine!

And, what about the conditions underfoot? Well, I have seen mud a foot deep and been faced with the prospect of winching the loads and lorries off-site. Boarding on and off sites was another tough job; trying to extricate 8 × 4 plywood boards when stuck in the mud was not easy, and with mud stuck on the underside they were quite heavy too. Also, filling in deep ruts and tamping down with a hefty piece of timber certainly dampens the spirits, and makes your arms ache!

Of course, the showmen often have to pay a 'bond' to the relevant authorities, which would be reserved for any damage to the ground. In such cases, the showmen all pull together and help one another to get the vehicles safely off and ready for the journey to the next event. Any damage or mud on the road would be resolved to hopefully get all of the bond returned.

Having worked with the showmen, I can only say what a good bunch of people they are. Like in other jobs, treat them right and they will be right with you. They will be one of the first to offer help in a crisis too. I remember one of our lads being over 100 miles from home when his mother was taken ill. Having no transport, a showman kindly offered his car so he could get home. That's the spirit and kindness that is typical of these fine people.

My experiences have mostly been with Warwick's, a Stoke-on-Trent operator; therefore, quite a few of the photographs in this book include their vehicles and they have been taken when attending their 'run' of fairs. However, I have travelled throughout the UK, so include photographs from some of the well-known fairs, including the Nottingham Goose Fair and the Great Dorset Steam Fair (GDSF). Other photographs include lorries seen in showmen's yards. Some may say that these photos are from the heyday of the travelling fairs, when good old British lorries were at the forefront.

Most of the known information is noted in the captions, as well as possible details. Also bear in mind that showmen are very adept at modifying vehicles to suit specific purposes, so the lorry you are viewing could have started life in a very different form.

The popularity of Gardner engined vehicles will be apparent. Therefore, it should be no surprise to find the book has a high selection of Foden, ERF and Atkinson lorries. Even when some of the lorries were retired, Gardner engines could often be put to use driving generators, the excellent fuel consumption and longevity being two very attractive and economical requirements.

And we have to remember that these vehicles had often served a previous life in road transport. A lot of the vehicles were purchased second-hand, and, as already mentioned, adapted by the showmen to their own particular specification.

I have tried to ensure that all facts are true, but sometimes with the passing of time things do get a bit hazy. Although a lot of photos were at the same fairs, these may appear randomly throughout the book rather than all grouped together, though this may actually prove more interesting reading.

If any facts are incorrect then it is entirely my own fault, and if your favourite operator or type of vehicle is not included, I can only apologise in advance. But if the reader enjoys looking at these photographs as much as I have enjoyed taking them then my work will have been well worth the effort.

To start the ball rolling, we go way back in time to show how things used to be. This FWD Model B is from the era of the First World War. Built in 1917, it went into use with R. Edwards & Sons Ltd from Swindon, Wiltshire. It was stored for many years along with a set of gallopers and is seen here on 31 March 2007 after being relocated to the Fairground Heritage Collection at Dingles, Lifton, Devon, which is well worth a visit.

Another exhibit at Dingles is this fine Atkinson eight-wheeler, complete with the Waltzer centre behind. Fleet No. 52 and affectionately named 'The Lion', it is from the famous fairground operator Anderton & Rowlands from Bristol and Plymouth.

Many AEC Matador lorries found their way onto the fairs. Originally built for the military, the four-wheel drive was very useful for soft ground, which was often encountered on the tobers. This one was owned by Harry Crooks and was seen at the Great Dorset Steam Fair in Tarrant Hinton on 3 September 1988.

Chassis No. 9394, an ERF 68GX (KV cab), was new to Hadyn Evans & Sons Ltd from Newport, Monmouthshire. Here it is in the ownership of Ken Shaw, who used it with his helter-skelter at the famous Nottingham Goose Fair in 1989.

This Foden Chinese 6 has now found its way into preservation with Knowles of Wimblington; however, it has been restored with an S20 cab. It is seen here at the Great Dorset Steam Fair on 3 September 1988 and it had an S21 'Mickey Mouse' cab fitted. My notes have it down as belonging to Cole's and that it was used with the Caterpillar ride, much favoured by courting couples!

At Ilkeston, Derbyshire, in 1988, this ageing ERF KV was spotted. It was owned by John Wesseldine. The street fair at Ilkeston is a popular event and even attracts showmen from the Continent. The ERF was seen after the event as the showmen were preparing to move on to the next fair.

After Nottingham Goose Fair on 4 October 1909, showing that the general public can be a little untidy! Here we see the giant Ferris wheel being pulled down with a helping hand from this MAN six-wheel crane. The modern rides get bigger and although manpower still reigns supreme, machines like this crane are now more commonplace.

The Forest Recreation Ground is the site for the annual Goose Fair. During the pull on is a good time to catch the vehicles arriving. This box van was one of many that had more or less got into position, ready for the build up, in 1988.

As mentioned earlier, the author worked for Warwick's for a number of years. This fine Foden S20 eight-wheeler, seen on Cheadle car park, was just being 'set' prior to build up in 1981. The long-standing September Cheadle Wakes Fair is nowadays held on the nearby recreation ground.

Affectionately known as 'My God' due to the registration number, this S21 (Mickey Mouse) cabbed four-wheeler was once with the Stoke-on-Trent hauliers M. F. Tyler. This is another photo from 1981 and was taken on the car park at Cheadle, Staffordshire, when the author had just shunted it up from the local industrial estate. Fleet No. 2.

The Brookhouse industrial estate, Cheadle, 1989. This Foden S39 eight-wheeler is loaded with dodgem plates on the bottom deck and overhead nets on the top. Warwick's no longer have this set of dodgems and have progressed to a modern fold-up trailer mounted dodgem ride.

A fine example of how showmen adapt vehicles to suit their needs. The previous owner of this Foden S81 was Malcolm Sample from the Sandbach area. He used it as a tractor unit, but it is seen here with 'work in progress' to convert it to a six-wheel tractor. Without any explanation, the body shows its origins. 1989.

The same vehicle just a few months later, having now been spray painted. It was on the Brookhouse industrial estate, Cheadle, Staffordshire, before moving into town ready to set up. The vehicle was used with an arcade, which has since been sold on.

Another of Warwick's seen in 1987 at Cheadle, Staffordshire, prior to painting. This Foden S83 transported the 'La Zig Zag' twist ride. This ride was 'old school' and labour intensive in building up. It was sold and they now have a more modern fold-up trailer mounted twist.

In the 1980s Warwick's had a paratrooper ride. It is seen here being built up with one of the two ex-Tilcon Mixers that the company had. Again seen on Cheadle car park, which was the author's hometown for many years, the photograph dates from 1982. This is another ride that has since been sold on.

This Foden with the 'Earth Shaker' Miami ride in tow was driven many times by the author, seen here in a lay-by, just outside Moreton-in-Marsh, in 2006. It is waiting for the 'all clear' to go into town for the build up. Although over the years many vehicle makes have been used, the company have always been a big fan of Foden lorries; in fact, the fleet is currently 100 per cent this marque. This lorry 'retired' the same year.

The author drove this Foden on a number of occasions. The vehicle is seen here in the yard after coming back from an event. Again, another ride that has been sold on is coupled behind the lorry – a 'mini' Waltzer. The vehicle, fleet No. 2, was still in use in 2023.

Fleet No. 1 was this S36 Foden, which is the legendary eight-wheeler that was retro-fitted with a Gardner 8LXB 240 bhp engine. For many years this vehicle carried the Waltzer platforms, cars, roof, etc. At the time the ride was known as the 'Whirlaround', and it is still with the family to this day. Over the years the ride has been modified and is now presented as the 'Nite Rider'. Cheadle, Staffordshire, 1982.

Here we can see the lorry with the ride at Hazel Grove, near Stockport. This event was one of a number where 'full flash' was fitted to the ride, this being all the roof rounding boards and shutters, etc. Since the photo was taken the ride has seen further improvements and the lorry has been retired.

This fine eight-wheeler is the current motive power for the Waltzer ride. It has a body that was built in-house and is complete with a lift-up roof. This makes things more comfortable when building up as you can keep the roof panels and, to a certain point, the staff under cover. Compare with the last photo where you can see the old system where staff got wet and the tarpaulin sheet was difficult to fit, especially in cold weather.

Another long-established fairground proprietor in the Stoke-on-Trent area is Stanworth's from Tunstall. Back in 1982, this ERF 68GX (LV) was seen on the Manor Road recreation ground in Fenton having built up the Waltzer. Stanworth's are big ERF users.

There is no mistaking which ride this lorry is carrying! Owned by George Pelham & Sons, this fine Atkinson eight-wheeler was at the Banbury Steam Society's annual rally at Bloxham. A well-established rally, it always has a good fairground section. This photograph dates back to 30 June 1991.

Going back a number of years (5 July 1993) a call was made to a fair in Ilminster, Devon. Although it has a Leyland badge, this AEC (possibly a Marshal) has a useful box van body. On the nearside a small generator can be seen with the exhaust rising up and above the top of the body to carry away the gases.

Leicestershire showmen J. Holland & Sons had this Scammell Routeman Mk 3 rigid eight-wheeler at the Nottingham Goose Fair in 1989. Originally it was a tanker with Shell-Mex. Note the front towing jaw and mirror at the top of the windscreen to assist when forward-shunting trailers.

Here we have another ex-Shell-Mex tanker. This one was at the annual Endon well dressing in 1990. Len Furborough travelled a big wheel with this outfit. The lorry was sold on and is now fully restored as a flat platform vehicle.

Just about visible on the headboard of this Foden S21 'Mickey Mouse' is the original owner's name. Baxter & Guion Ltd were a potato merchant from Peterborough, but the vehicle was seen in retirement in a showmen's yard near the Staffordshire/Cheshire border in 2000.

Another vehicle that was with George Pelham & Sons dodgems at the Banbury rally was this Foden S40. The cab is all steel and made by Motor Panels, who supplied cabs to many manufacturers. Unfortunately, these cabs did suffer badly from corrosion.

Still retaining the original wheelbase, this Seddon Atkinson 301 would originally have been a tractor unit. Now fitted with a box van body, the vehicle was seen at the annual May Fair in Bakewell, Derbyshire, in 2013. Again, these cabs were manufactured by Motor Panels.

Nottingham Goose Fair has set arrival times for the pull on. Consequently, it's not unusual to spot lorries parked close to the city, waiting for the allocated time. This ex-Pickford's 6 × 4 Atkinson Venturer of Bob Wilson from Birmingham was in a lay-by near Toton back in 1988.

Chassis No. 49796 is a 25C3 ERF C Series with a Kirkstall double-drive rear bogie. Possibly new to KPC, it is seen in its later guise with John Stevens as a travelling shooting gallery. This was on Stafford Common on 28 April 1991.

Not a great many BMC Lairds were to be seen on the fair. This one had just pulled onto the Goose Fair site in Nottingham (1988) and was heading for the caravan park. At the time, vehicles arriving here were directed left for caravans, and right or straight on for the rides.

In exceptional condition in 1988 at Ashbourne, Derbyshire, was this fine Foden DG of Chapmans. It travelled with a coconut shy and is thought to be an ex-army vehicle. Parked behind the stalls, the vehicle is on ground that typifies some fairground sites.

Ex-Wrekin Roadways as a tractor unit. This Foden S39 has been rebuilt to represent a typical showman's tractor. It is very often seen at vintage rallies with a smart showman's living van in tow. On this occasion it faced the camera in a showmen's yard near Stoke-on-Trent in 2005.

Alexis Elizabeth of John Neal & Son is their fine Atkinson with the Mk 1 cab. It is seen here in Nottingham at the Goose Fair pull on in 1988. Visible in the foreground are the blocks that the staff are getting set for the lorry to mount to keep the vehicle level when generating.

This Foden lorry (S10 Mk 3 cab) is in the same registration sequence as the one that the author drove for Warwick's. Both are ex-cement mixers. With double-drive bogies, they are the ideal vehicle for the showmen. This one was at the annual fair in the picturesque valley at Brabyns Park, Marple, in the Greater Manchester borough of Stockport.

Peter Manning used this fine-looking Foden S21 eight-wheeler with his Caterpillar ride. Most readers will know that the S21 cab earned the nickname 'Mickey Mouse'. Keen-eyed readers will see the vehicle has been 'scotched' behind the drive axle, just to be on the safe side!

Ilkeston fair in Derbyshire has a tradition of seeing a small number of showmen coming over from the Continent. This Mercedes 1624 had been left ticking over to build up the air reservoirs before departing for home. The 'haze' of exhaust means it hadn't quite warmed up.

And again, another Continental showman. The exhaust gives away the fact that this left-hand drive DAF 3300 with drawbar trailer was warming up and getting ready for departure.

One of a pair at the Tern Valley Vintage rally at Market Drayton on 18 September 1988 was Wright's Foden S36 eight-wheeler. Fleet No. 2, *Emma*, certainly looked the part. The gap in the front of the Luton van body is to give clearance when tilting the cab.

A classic view of building up at the Llandudno Victorian Extravaganza on 2 May 2014. The ERF EC10 clearly shows its original owners as Ashfield Hauliers (John Wright) of Sutton in Ashfield. The gaff lad is taking the opportunity for a quick swig of his energy drink – a staple requirement on this sort of work!

Astle Park Traction Engine Rally 2011. This Irish-registered Foden 4275 (sleeper cab) fleet No. 2 of Howards from Kirk Ireton, Derbyshire, is pictured parked on one side waiting for the rally to end. The dismantling of the steam gallopers that they own would see it getting loaded ready for the next event.

And now for No. 3 in the Howards' fleet. This well-presented ERF EC14 tractor unit is also at Astle Park. It is situated next to the 'Atlantic Star' big wheel for generating purposes. Again, it shows the vehicle sitting on wooden blocks to keep it level while generating.

Morley's from New Mills, near Stockport, are long-established fairground operators. This Foden FG is now actually in preservation. It contains living quarters, a kitchen and bathroom. It was also used to tow a trailer, which was the bedroom. To this day the vehicle still has the bath in situ.

There is no mistaking what this vehicle is promoting. With massive, chromed letters on the side, this ERF EC10 is unmistakably one of Armstrong's vehicles that is used with the dodgems. The men are removing the dodgem plates after the Goose Fair had finished.

John Collins is a regular visitor to Leek, a small market town in the Staffordshire Moorlands. Seen having just arrived on the High Street car park is his smart Foden Alpha Mk 2 with the trailer-mounted Miami ride. 19 November 2021.

Another vehicle that has been pressed into service before getting repainted was with Perrin Prints, *Superbob*. The unit is an ex-Shell Foden 4350. It is a single drive, twin-steer tractor and is caught on camera just threading its way through the rides to find its position at the Goose Fair in 2009.

Sporting airbrushed pictures of some famous football players was this ERF E6 (rest cab) down at the Marple Fair on 19 June 2005. The vehicle is a self-contained funhouse and had yet to be built up. Other rides can be seen already built up in the background. Also seen is the author's Miami paybox 'office'.

Not to be confused with the A Series ERF, here we have a 64G that has had a more modern LV (7LV) cab fitted. The underslung rear springs are a main identifying feature of the pre-A Series. The vehicle was located on Stafford Common in 1991.

Another ex-Shell Mex BP Scammell in service with a showman at Nottingham Goose Fair. It is a Scammell Routeman Mk 3 and has a sizeable Luton van body. Mounted on the offside is a generator set, again showing how showmen adapt their vehicles.

Nottingham pull on back in 1988, and we have here a Leyland Super Comet lorry and drawbar trailer. The Sankey-made 'Ergomatic' cab was holding up reasonably well with only minor rust showing. It is interesting to see the oil drum mounted high above the cab, possibly holding fuel for a generator.

Another vehicle, this time seen in 2009, packing up after the Goose Fair has ended. The smart ERF EC11 (rest cab) has the 'Wacky Playtruck' attached, which is being loaded into the step van box van trailer. Note the track that has been laid to make traversing the ground easier.

Anthony Harris from Brownhills trades and uses the famous Pat Collins name, and always presents a fine fleet of vehicles. This Foden S39 eight-wheeler had just arrived at Nottingham in 1988. Unfortunately, *Dan Baker* fleet No. 1 was sadly lost when it was destroyed in a fire.

Articulated outfits have a distinct advantage when it comes to moving loads around, by sheer virtue of being able to swap trailers. This ERF EC10 with sleeper cab is first seen in 2003 at Stafford Common with a trailer loaded with fencing. Note the name *Colin* and fleet number of 14.

The same vehicle seen in a different year, once more on Stafford Common but this time coupled to a box van trailer. Keen-eyed readers will notice a few changes, including the fleet number (6) and the name *Relentless*.

The name *Dan Baker* was resurrected for this Foden 4380 heavy generating tractor. Fleet No. 8 was originally a tractor unit with James Booth of Westhoughton, near Bolton, and would have been used with a tipping trailer. Another well-turned-out vehicle and a credit to the company.

This is one of two consecutively registered ERF B Series lorries that Anthony Harris owned, the other being FRY 389V. Both were new to Moores of Ashby as 4 × 2 units. Converted into heavy 6 × 4 tractors, this one, *Elias Joseph* (1), was again seen on Stafford Common in 1991.

How about this for a line up?! Right at the back is FRY 388V, which at the time was still in the throes of conversion and minus the company livery. Then FRY 389V (2) is showing its face before fleet Nos 4 and 5, which are in the foreground.

John Farrar, from Sheffield, had this fine Foden 4350 (1) at the 2009 Goose Fair. It is coupled up to the trailer-mounted fold-up dodgem set. These modern fold-up rides certainly save some time with the build up and pulling down times.

Astle Park Traction Engine Rally saw this traditional old favourite, the Wall of Death ride, on site. Providing traction was this smart ERF EC11, complete with a rear-mounted crane; it would be a great asset in building up the ride. Originally this would have been a tractor unit. The Wall of Death is certainly a must-see ride!

Jan De Koning's King Swing ride behind his Foden Alpha Mk 2 six-wheel unit at Llandudno. It was just getting 'set', ready for the Llandudno Victorian Extravaganza. This ride is one of the many new white-knuckle rides now appearing on the fairs.

Another John Stevens vehicle, this time an ERF 68GX or 68GXB depending on whether it has a Gardner 150 (6LX) or a Gardner 180 (6LXB) engine. Again, this was with the Pat Collins fair on Stafford Common in 1991.

It was 1982 and this Guy Warrior of Frankie Warwick was on the old site of Cheadle Wakes Fair before it was moved to the local recreation ground. The 'Invincible' badge will be an addition off another Guy lorry. The lorry normally towed the living van, which is located just behind.

Another of the Warwick family was William, or 'Billy' as he was known. He travelled another old-time ride, the Skid, which used to be very popular. This Foden S21 'Mickey Mouse' was originally owned by Sellars and Kent from Ilam, Derbyshire.

Billy Warwick's other 'Mickey Mouse' Foden was also used alongside the previous motor to travel the Skid. This one was new to Rugby Cement as their fleet No. 495. Both vehicles are seen on Cheadle car park in 1982 after travelling over from Selston, Nottingham.

Still travelling the Skid ten years later, Billy Warwick had pensioned off the S21 Mickey Mouse Fodens, with one of the replacements being this ERF B Series eight-wheeler. Seen in Billy's home county, the ERF had been loaded with the Skid cars after the annual Goose Fair.

Two Fodens of Kurt Hill from Bolton, a Mk 1 Alpha artic on the right and a 3,000 Series eight-wheeler with the narrow S10 cab on the left. Both lorries were at the Astle Park Traction Engine Rally in 2014 with the proprietor's Waltzer ride.

This ex-Harrison & Jones Foden S80 has a special elevating roof that was used on the Recitel contract to carry foam – the foam blocks were compressed by lowering the roof once loaded. The vehicle passed into showland and was seen at Market Drayton's vintage rally in 1988.

The unmistakeable iron latticework in the background gives this shot away as the Brighton seafront on Madeira Drive. The 'gaff lads' seem to be waiting to finish loading this ERF 68GX. The author was attending the HVCS London–Brighton run in 1987 at the time.

The Bedford TM was never a major contender in the UK, even less so finding use on the fairgrounds. Looking at the wheelbase on this box van, it can safely be assumed to have originally been a tractor unit. Nottingham Goose fair site, 1989.

Holland's Leyland Octopus was looking a little 'work worn' when photographed at Nottingham in 1989. Motor Panels' LAD 'waterfall' cab showing the usual 'tin worm'. Luckily, this vehicle was saved and is now restored in the livery of British Road Services.

Stanley Reeves & Son travelled this funhouse behind a 'Mickey Mouse' Foden S21 four-wheeler. It was parked near to Ilkeston after the fair had finished getting ready for the next gaff in 1988. The S21 was a popular choice for a number of showmen.

A number of showmen are often offered ground by the lessees of established fairs. This Atkinson Borderer of Charles Bryant was one such visitor to the annual Cheadle (Staffordshire) Wakes Fair, which is traditionally held in September. The trailer-mounted ride is a Satellite.

Chassis No. 8709 is an ERF 44G (KV) and was new to Leonard Green Haulage Ltd in 1958. Later on it entered showman's use with Ernie Chapman of Wymeswold, Leicestershire. This photo was taken at the Goose Fair in 1992 and it was seen still working in 2000 – not bad for a vehicle that was forty-two years old!

This eight-wheel B Series ERF (fleet No. 50) is part of the famous Anderton & Rowlands outfit. It is seen having a rest with the Ski-Jump ride just off the A30 at Sourton Cross in Devon one Sunday morning. The vehicle was new to Frank Tucker and ran in the Tarmac-Westbrick livery.

Ron Taylor was famous for his boxing booth with a cry of, 'A fiver for the winner, a good hiding for the loser.' However, this Guy Big J4 contained a fun house and is seen at the Hanley Central Forest Park fair back in 1991. Ron sadly passed away in his home town of Gloucester in 2006 aged ninety-five.

When on a South West 'safari' a call was made to the small village of Puddletown in Dorset. On station was C. T. Cole & Sons from Southampton. This ERF 66GX had just pulled on the ground with a ride paybox in tow.

Puddletown again and Cole's ERF B Series tractor pulled on with two trailers in tow, which is allowed for showmen. The vehicle would have originally been a tractor unit, but was kitted out with generator sets to provide power for the rides.

Twenty-seven years old at the time, this Seddon of Cole's was still working well. These few photos at Puddletown were taken on 6 July 1993. Towing a box van trailer, the vehicle was also used for powering the rides and had two generators on board. The lorry did carry on in service into the 2000s.

Cole's tidy ERF B Series eight-wheeler. This was well loaded, with the dodgem plates on the bottom platform and the cars on the next two decks of the specially made body. The tarpaulin cover has been placed on the front top deck ready for unloading. It is also towing a fold-up juvenile ride.

Harry Wigfield was born in Armroyd Lane, Elsecar, South Yorkshire. From an early age he developed an interest in fairgrounds. This interest led Harry to buy various fairground rides, which he travelled for a number of years along with the Enston Bros. This Enston Bros Atkinson was one of many vehicles used, and is seen alongside the famous Royal Coronation Speedway at Astle Park rally in 1990.

Enston Bros ERF B Series at Grappenhall, Warrington, on 2 August 1992. Of note is that the Harry Wigfield/Enston Bros used the same livery on their lorries. A livery that seemed to find favour after the purchase of an ex-Pollock of Mussleburgh Atkinson, which came along with the Royal Coronation Speedway from Crows, showmen from Northallerton.

This is the lorry as bought from Crows by Armroyd Lane, an Atkinson Mk 1 eight-wheeler. The tartan sash and Telstar name was retained from the Pollock days. This too was in attendance at the Astle Park rally in 1990.

Another of Armroyd Lane's vehicles at Grappenhall was this Foden S80 eight-wheel lorry, which is fitted with a useful crane. Unfortunately, the vehicle has suffered some minor damage to the cab – it happens! The Ford D Series box van to the left was replaced by a DAF 2100 in 1996.

This Atkinson Borderer had retained its tractor unit wheelbase but was fitted with a box van body when seen at Grappenhall powering the Coronation Speedway. The name *Elsecar* was allocated to this lorry as a tribute to Harry's birthplace.

This fine Atkinson Mk 1 was purchased as a chassis cab from Gordon Pearson of Ibstock, Leicestershire. This body was constructed in house by Armroyd Lane Amusements. It had useful storage 'belly' boxes and racks for oil drum storage.

And, as if by magic, we see the same lorry when in service with Gordon Pearson in 1984. This was at a small fair in the village of Barrow upon Soar, Leicestershire. This field is actually prone to severe flooding by the River Soar, but luckily not on this occasion. Note the different body style.

Keeping company with the Atkinson was a vehicle not often seen on the fairs: a Commer VC, which was also with Gordon Pearson. With the lettering on the side of the Luton van there is no mistaking the type of ride it supported. Barrow upon Soar, 1984.

Another relatively rare vehicle to be seen on the fairs was the Albion CH3 'Chieftain', which was a lightweight four-wheel model with a four-cylinder engine. This particular vehicle would have been close to the end of production, which ended in 1967. Arthur Fossett used this with his shooter at the Goose Fair on 4 October 1992.

Tony Marchington was behind the Buxworth Steam Group and at one time he also owned the *Flying Scotsman* locomotive. This Atkinson Defender eight-wheeler was on Hartington Moor, Derbyshire, where a vintage fair was held. The vehicle is towing a steam-operated ride centre. Note the fold-down chimney.

Between fairs and taking a breather was Terry Atha's S83 eight-wheeler with the 'kip' behind. This was used with the Hellblazer Waltzer ride. No doubt the staff were seeking refreshments and a comfort break on the M62 Birch Service area when seen on 2 June 1994.

Parked on the Barnfields industrial estate in Leek, Staffordshire, was Arthur William Price's B Series ERF. Behind is a compact trailer-mounted Meteorite or Round Up ride. The outfit was seen in May 1991.

In 1989 the author was down in Chichester to collect a kit car. Having loaded it up, a showmen's yard was spotted and a quick venture into it saw a few vehicles parked up. This AEC Matador, which looked in good order, had a crane mounted on the back – a useful vehicle to have around the yard.

The old Victoria ground of Stoke City FC was the setting for this ERF six-wheeler (LV cab) of Jennings Brothers from Kidderminster. A limited number of fairs were held on this site in the early 1990s. The lorry was in attendance with the owner's big wheel.

Just swinging around, ready to set the living van at the 1989 Goose Fair, is Jimmy Whiting's 'Mickey Mouse' Foden S21 six-wheel box van. The body is fitted with sliding side doors, which give good access to the load.

Manchester showman Glyn De Koning attended a small fair in Stoke with this Atkinson Defender eight-wheeler on the old Minton Hollins pottery site in 1992. Not long after, the site was regenerated and became part of the Caudwell mobile phone empire.

What some may consider to be 'bling' is the generous amount of chrome on Raymond Armstrong's Scammell Handyman Mk 2 and, indeed, on the living van too. Note the 'pull out' on the side of the living van to provide additional internal space. It is set up for the duration of the Goose Fair in 1989.

Smiths of Doncaster had this well-kept ERF LV van seen at Nottingham in 1992. Chassis No. 14668 was built as a 5.4G, which had a Gardner 5LW engine; however, the grille badge is for a 120 bhp engine, which is the 6LW, so it may have been re-engined.

A very tidy Mk 1 Atkinson of Richard Strickland, Stoke-on-Trent. It had just pulled onto the old site of Cheadle Wakes Fair on the town centre car park. This was back in 1982 before the car park was altered by the local council, making it difficult to hold the fair there.

Once the fair is set up it can be difficult to get decent photographs of the lorries. They are often hemmed in, like this AEC six-wheeler that was spotted at the Great Dorset Steam Fair at Tarrant Hinton in 1988. The frame has been built over what seems to have been a dropside body as the hinge pins are still in situ.

From the neighbouring county of Hampshire, this Foden S39 six-wheel box van had crossed the county line for the GDSF in 1988. C. Burnett are from the market town of Waterlooville, which is near Havant, a distance of only 60 miles away.

Central Forest Park in Hanley, Stoke-on-Trent, is a reclaimed piece of land transformed from a former pit spoil tip, namely Hanley Deep Pit. Fairs have been held on the site for many years and this Leyland Comet box van was visiting in May 1991.

A visit to Kings Park in Bournemouth was undertaken on 4 September 1988 to see the start of the HCVS Bournemouth to Bath run. There was a fair on site at the time, which included this Foden S39. Retaining its tractor unit wheelbase, a small platform body has been fitted to accommodate a generator and a couple of fuel drums.

A Rolls-Royce-powered Foden S83 eight-wheeler of Bert Holland of Wigston, Leicester, is seen here on full lock on the Goose Fair site having unhitched its trailer. The pull-on day is always a busy time and lots of like-minded enthusiasts are often vying for pole position to obtain a good photo. Patience and some good foot slogging is the order of the day!

Another vehicle preparing to depart the 1992 Goose Fair was this 1970-registered AEC Mercury with a box van body. It is in the living van area, so no doubt will be coupling up prior to setting off to the next venue.

As previously mentioned, it is not always easy to get photos at some events. This vehicle is reputedly the longest Atkinson Defender ever built and was new to Jack Henley of Spelmonden, Kent. It was used on general haulage before finding its way to B. Cole & Sons from Southampton. It was captured hemmed in at the GDSF on 3 September 1988.

Taken on the same date as the previous photo, this Seddon box van was somewhat rare on the grounds. At a guess it is possibly a 16:4 model; however, it was not unknown for tractor units to be converted, in which case it could be a 32:4 model. These vehicles had a version of the Motor Panels cab fitted.

Looking more like a general haulage outfit, this Bedford TM John Crick was at the Nottingham Goose Fair in 1992 with a 40-foot ISO container on the trailer. Minus a front panel, it is obviously an ex-Schweppes tractor unit that has been pressed into service.

According to some sources this Foden S21 'Mickey Mouse' was new to Tilcon. Prior to leaving the fair at Ilkeston in 1988, it was getting a 'top up' of diesel from one of the gaff lads before setting off. The owner, Alicia White, stands by holding the 'tun dish'.

Ilminster Fair again in 1993 and a well-presented Atkinson of Wynn's Amusements is pulling on with the Waltzer. The vehicle has a couple of 'truck' accessories of the day, namely a set of air horns mounted on the body and the chrome 'Haulin Ass' logo on the front grille.

This Leyland Octopus with Ergomatic cab was new to Kings of Chelmsford, Essex, as a tipper. Rebodied, as seen, as a double-deck frame with enclosed sides, it was another vehicle at Kings Park, Bournemouth, Hampshire, on 4 September 1988.

Registered in Staffordshire, which is the author's home county, it was always interesting to see 'local' vehicles, albeit many miles away at Puddletown, Dorset. This Scammell Handyman Mk 2 still retains its tractor unit wheelbase but was in service with Chipperfield's as a generator tractor.

Carrying the camera when out and about often resulted in snaps of unexpected vehicles. Spotted when doing casual lorry driving was this Foden S106 (S10 Mk 3 cab) six-wheel box van complete with living van in tow. It was parked up on the Barnfields industrial estate in Leek, Staffordshire, on 15 May 1991.

Another vehicle that has survived and is now in preservation is this ex-Marley Tiles Atkinson 'bow front' eight-wheeler. A feature of these Marley Atkinsons was the wide radiator and the raised figures seen on the cab side, which was the fleet number. It had been retired when seen here in the owner's yard at Chickerell, Weymouth.

Also in Townsend's at Chickerell on the same visit (4 April 1991) was this ERF 68GX with a frame-type body. It is an early example with the Jennings long door cab. This too had been retired. Unfortunately, the outcome of this particular vehicle is not known.

In 1985 at a small village fair in Blythe Bridge, Stoke-on-Trent, was this Mk 1 Atkinson eight-wheel van with sliding side doors. It was in attendance with the ride behind, which is a Round Up or, as some people call them, 'Meteorite'.

Another in the Stoke-on-Trent area, this time at Manor Road, Fenton, where this Foden S34 Luton van of Richard Cooney & Son was part of the Stanworth's May fair, which is held every year. The front panel of the body lifts up to allow space for the lorry cab to tilt.

Another Luton van is featured here. This one was in the town centre at Congleton, Cheshire. It is based on a Leyland Comet chassis. The cab is a rare all-aluminium example that was built by A. Holmes of Preston and known as a Homalloy.

Attingham Park, Shrewsbury, 25 May 1986, and a vintage rally was held at this National Trust-owned property. A small fair was also in attendance, and, again, at the time a comparatively rare vehicle on the fairs were the BMC FFK lorries. This one was badged as a Morris.

A good example of a vehicle that has been pressed into service still wearing its original livery. This Seddon removals van was also at Attingham Park in 1986. It is interesting to see that there is an area over the cab that provides sleeping quarters, the ladder seemingly being the means of access.

A very smart-looking and well-turned-out Foden S80 eight-wheeler with a large Luton van body. This was seen at the small fair at Barrow upon Soar, Leicestershire, back in 1984. It is hard to believe when looking through the slide collection that this was taken forty years ago!

Charles Sketchley's Foden S80 is certainly eye-catching in this bright livery. It is seen having pulled onto the Goose Fair site in 1988 with his Meteorite in tow. The exhaust up the side of the van body gives away the fact that a generator is mounted inside.

This ex-military Albion CX22 artillery gun tractor was in fact just 'out of service' with Shaw's Amusements. It was entered as an exhibit in the spring rally at the Leyland Museum on 25 May 1986. Apart from non-standard mirrors and the indicators atop the front wings, it is very original; however, it is minus the canvas cover over the hoops of the body.

Being checked in at Nottingham by the police constable seen on the left is this ERF 68GX eight-wheeler. All vehicles are monitored onto the Goose Fair site and, as previously mentioned, they have arrival time slots that have to be adhered to, thus avoiding traffic congestion.

En route to Retford to see the late Keith Hudson, who had done a fairground lorry painting for the author. This Foden S39 was encountered in a lay-by not far from the town. Apparently, the fair had recently been in the town and this outfit was obviously awaiting movement to the next venue.

This AEC Mercury was originally with Bees of Hinckley, Leicestershire, who were parcel distribution specialists – the distinctive front bumper arrangement is the giveaway! This one found its way onto the fairs and was seen in 1986 at Central Forest Park, Hanley.

In the town centre at Retford in 1990 is this Foden S83, which presumably was originally a tractor unit. It was one of the last vehicles to leave after the fair had been pulled down. The gaff lads were spotted doing the last round of litter picking, etc., prior to departure.

Lancashire showman J. E. Silcock from Warrington had this magnificent Atkinson and drawbar trailer at the 1982 Astle Park Traction Engine Rally. As the very bold writing on the sign depicts, it was used to transport the dodgem track and cars.

On a 'safari' in the North East with a couple of other like-minded enthusiasts on 30 May 1993, this ERF 64G (LV) Luton van was spotted in a yard at Wolsingham, County Durham. L. Cooper & Son are based approximately 17 miles away from Wolsingham at Ferryhill, County Durham.

The unmistakable sound of a Leyland 680 engine heard at Nottingham in 1989 saw the author following this Foden S21 (Mickey Mouse) until it found its position on the fairground. Used with a ghost train ride, this ex-Blue Circle Cement lorry was later very fortunate to be saved for preservation.

Yet another vehicle parked in a lay-by after departing from the Retford fair in 1990. This Foden S83 still retains its original owner's headboard, Jeffries Transport Ltd of Otley, Yorkshire. At one time big Foden users, this one was being given a further lease of life on the fairs.

Thomas Cooper from Stoke-on-Trent had this ex-Great Universal Stores (GUS) AEC Mercury in use on the fairs. As it has a Worcestershire registration it may have been allocated to the Kays of Worcester mail order catalogue concern, which were part of GUS. It was captured on film in the Stoke area in 1986.

Back in 1990, fleet No. 3 of John Collins from Manchester was this ERF 68GX eight-wheeler. Photographed on the Leek cattle market site, it can be seen with a trailer coupled up to the front towing pin, which many showmen find is useful for 'nosing in' to confined spaces.

His Majesty of Tommy Green from Lancashire making a royal entrance at the 1989 Nottingham Goose Fair pull on. Normally with the flying coaster ride, this was one of two Leyland Octopus lorries that he had. This lorry is another that is now safe in the hands of a preservationist.

This Atkinson Mk 1 was in very tidy condition considering it was seventeen years old when spotted at the May fair, Manor Road, Fenton, Stoke-on-Trent, in 1983. Owned by Ken Simons & Son, they were another lessee of Stanworth's, a local Stoke-on-Trent fairground proprietor.

Having managed to avoid the Alsatian in the last photo, the author took a snap of this Mk 1 Atkinson, which was also at Manor Road, Fenton, in 1983. Maybe it was owned by Ken Simons too? Interesting to see that the van body on this is ex-Kwik Save, a supermarket chain that had its origins in North Wales.

Another shot from Nottingham in 1992 that shows the amount of litter left behind by punters! James Bond from Lutterworth had this ERF B Series *Heavy Locomotive* eight-wheeler van on site. It is seen getting ready for departure and the paintwork certainly catches the eye.

Sometimes when trying to place a ride on your allocated spot the conditions underfoot can thwart progress. Helping hands are never far away, though, and here we see Ronnie Weston from Rhyl with his Foden S24 helping a Scammell Crusader into position at Nottingham in 1988.

J. Whiting with the Chaser ride pulling onto Nottingham Goose Fair in 1989 with his Foden S21 ('Mickey Mouse') eight-wheeler. The ride centre is behind on the trailer. A generator is seen on the lorry and also a gantry crane for lifting off the ride platforms.

Endon, in Stoke-on-Trent, is a small village that holds a traditional well dressing event, usually held on the May bank holiday weekend. Part of the celebrations include a fun fair, and this Foden with an S10 Mk 1 cab was parked near the site prior to building up in 1990.

These odd-looking vehicles were partially designed by British Road Services, who indeed took most of the production. They were affectionately known as 'Noddy' vans. This one found its way onto the fairs and was captured on film at Elvaston Castle Steam Rally in 1988.

Going back to the early 1980s there were still a number of elderly vehicles to be seen on the fairs. Here we have a 1959 Thornycroft Swiftsure van of C. Holland from Sileby in Leicestershire. Photographed at Rempstone Rally in 1983 when just a mere twenty-four years old.

En route to collect a production machine in the Greater Manchester area, the author travelled through Hyde where a fair was seen. On site were a number of vehicles. This eight-wheel Scammell Routeman Mk 3 frame lorry was reversed up to the dodgem track ready for when the ride was to be pulled down.

Also at Hyde was this Foden S80 four-wheel van, which had a stall built up on the side or, as it is known by the fairground fraternity, a 'joint'. The amount of litter points to the fair having been open for a number of days, in what seems to be typical Manchester weather – rain!

Hyde again, this time way back in 1989. Here we see Michael Mulhearn's Foden S39 'Sixer' lorry, which housed the generators, hence 'Power Plant' being written on the front. As can be seen from the address, Mulhearn's were local to the area.

Another ex-Blue Circle Cement lorry that had an extended life on the fair. Another Foden S21 'Mickey Mouse' that was at a small fair in Newcastle-under-Lyme in 1986. The lorry was in semi-retirement for a while, but went to numerous rallies before going back to the fairs again.

Another lorry in Retford just before departing to the next event was this Atkinson Mk 1 four-wheel van of W. Goodman from Doncaster. In very tidy condition for its age (twenty-six years) the vehicle typifies a showman's vehicle with a belly box under the body and a rack housing a spare drum of fuel.

Another outfit that was not easy to photograph was this Foden S36 artic just outside Retford. The artic was in a lay-by and just to the left was another vehicle, which was blocking off the rest of the trailer. Oh well, you win some, you lose some.

Tommy Lovett and his funhouse with living van in tow, pulling onto the Goose Fair in 1989. A Stoke-on-Trent-registered ERF with an early Jennings LV cab, which no doubt would have been supplied by Stoke dealers Beech's Garage. Most likely it is a cut down eight-wheeler.

In 1990 while travelling through Trentham on the A34, it was something of a surprise to spot this outfit. The owner is thought to be Billy Holden. The AEC Marshal is loaded with a Waltzer ride and looks to have once been a dropside lorry as the hinges are still on the body.

The *Leicester Mercury* held a transport festival at Abbey Park, Leicester, for a number of years and a fair also attended. What is thought to be Tommy Connell's Guy Big J4 was there on 22 May 1988. The tractor has the generator sets on board and a box van trailer in tow.

The sleeper cab version on this Foden is known as the S81 and was normally fitted to heavy haulage tractor units. Michael Wallis had two such vehicles at Leek, Staffordshire, in 1990. This one, 'The M56 Flyer', was used with his Ski Jump ride.

Michael Wallis's other Foden S81 at the Leek cattle market ground. This one was in the Ghostbusters livery, with just a small MW in the roundel indicating ownership (both vehicles had the roundel). Also, the two units had the eight-cylinder Gardner 8LXB 240 bhp engine fitted. This one was 'The M62 Flyer'.

Today fold-up, self-contained, trailer-mounted loads are more popular on the fairs. However, M. Herbert had this ERF B Series (chassis No. 40967) at Ilminster on 5 July 1993 with his paratrooper ride. At the time *Proud Mary* was certainly looking very smart.

Also at Ilminster, and at the same time, was this well-worked AEC Mammoth Major eight-wheeler. This one was logged as belonging to Lewis Herbert and typifies the way things were done, with parts of the ride and spare fuel drums on board. The Sankey cab is certainly showing signs of the dreaded 'tin worm' and has a temporary patch showing on the wing.

With parts of a Waltzer ride on the double-deck frame body, this ERF B Series eight-wheeler will be lined up ready to complete the build up of the ride in the background. David Wynn had this at Ilminster on a nice, fine day – the gaff lads would be pleased doing the building up.

Banbury Steam Rally on the Friday preceding the event (28 June 1991) and John Hatwell & Sons was building up his juvenile rides. His very smart Atkinson Mk 1 *The Cotswold Queen* had almost finished unloading and was ready for the weekend fun to begin.

The annual steam rally at Astle Park has had a fair section for many years. This Foden S80 tractor had been used for shunting trailers in a much-favoured way by nosing them into position. This allows the driver better vision and is a little easier than reversing. 11 August 1990.

This Scammell Mk 3 Handyman was in William Butlin's yard, near Oxford. It is another vehicle in use as a four-wheel van that would have originally been a tractor unit. It proudly displays on the front of the cab 'Showmans Special', which no doubt it is!

Back to Abbey Park, Leicester, in 1988 for the *Leicester Mercury* event. We have another ex-Great Universal Stores AEC Mercury. The company had a number of these Luton vans used on mail order catalogue distribution. Unfortunately, the showman owner was not established.

Tagging onto Stanworth's fair at Central Forest Park, Hanley, in 1989 was Joe Swift with this Atkinson Borderer. According to the radiator badge it is a Cummins engine version. It is another ex-tractor unit with a van body built on what is the original wheelbase.

John Collins's Atkinson Defender eight-wheeler actually has a fifth wheel mounted at the rear of the chassis to couple up to the lift up paratrooper ride – quite a sight when on the road. No. 1 is parked in a corner of Leek cattle market, well away from the crowds when generating.

Mr Plod seems to be setting off to check the paperwork for the entry of this tidy Foden S24 six-wheeler at Nottingham Goose Fair. It is facing the right way to set the living van that's in tow, the little boy in the cab presumably eager to get settled in for the duration.

If anyone asks what a typical showman's lorry is then you could probably get no better than this fine machine. This eight-wheel Foden S21 ('Mickey Mouse') of Shaw's Amusements has it all: a good-sized body with side skirts, generator across the back and a nice paint job complete with a fleet number – magic!

Albert Proctor was a big fan of the Atkinson marque, with several turning up at the Goose Fair in 1989. This Mk 1 six-wheeler had been set more or less in position for the build up on pull-on day. The gaff lad in the background was no doubt contemplating the forthcoming graft.

Another of Albert Proctor's Mk 1 Atkinson six-wheelers, this one being fully sign written and advertising the fact that it's connected with the company's Waltzer ride. It is also towing the ride centre. Nottingham, 1989.

A well worked ERF B Series (along with an AEC in the background) was spotted in a lay-by near to Ilminster, Devon, on 5 July 1993. Both were eight-wheelers and both were well loaded. The ERF chassis number, 38462, was originally registered in Lincolnshire.

Yet another ex-tractor unit converted to a box van, this AEC is possibly a Mandator. With no name on the vehicle, it could not be determined who the owner was. It was seen on 27 March 1993 on Stafford Common along with lessees, Anthony Harris's fair.

Back to Ilminster in 1993 and we see here a Guy Big J4T, another converted tractor unit. This one is possibly ex-British Telecom or London Carriers as both companies had quite a number of these. Again, typical of a Motor Panels cab, the rust is setting in.

Thirty-four years ago at Nottingham it was not unusual to see some of the older vehicles still in service. This Commer VC box van with a Perkins engine was seventeen years old then, but was still looking in good order. The roller shutter door on the side would be useful when loading/unloading.

Another vehicle taking a break on the Barnfields industrial estate in Leek, Staffordshire, was this ERF B Series eight-wheeler and 'kip' in tow. Although a number of vehicles were on site, there was no staff around to glean any other information. 15 May 1991.

Henry Herbert bought this trailer-mounted lift-up paratrooper ride in 1992. The following year it was seen parked in a lay-by at Ilminster. The Foden S39 is certainly a mean-looking machine without rear mudguards.

Atkinson Mk 1 six-wheel unit of Billy Danter, which, according to records, is an ex-Marley Tiles cut-down eight-wheeler, possibly run by a sub-contractor (S. Johnston). Fleet No. 4 was between fairs and in a lay-by on the A38 just south of Birmingham in 1985.

1989 and this Foden S80 six-wheel van was looking a little work worn at Normacot Fair in Stoke-on-Trent. However, twelve months later at the same venue it had been afforded a repaint and looked a lot tidier.

This fine ERF 68GX was originally a flat platform lorry with Rugby Cement. It was fleet No. 697 and was based at Southam Works. It passed to Lol Bishton and was used with his gallopers. Somewhere along the line it has gained a Foden front bumper. Nottingham, 1989.

Sporting a 'cherished' number plate, which had been transferred from an earlier Foden, this Foden 4325 in service with J. E. Silcock was still sporting its previous owner's name and livery. It was seen at the Astle Park rally on 13 August 2011.

'Truck of the Year' was first introduced in 1977. Sponsored by *Truck* magazine, it was instigated by the late Pat Kennett. The first vehicle to receive the accolade was the Seddon Atkinson 200. This example was seen at the cattle market pull on prior to the fair at Leek, Staffordshire, in 1990.

Another lorry at Leek at the same time was this Atkinson Searcher, which was the name given to the Mk 2 six-wheel vehicles with the dummy radiator grille. The proclamation on the headboard leaves no doubt about what the vehicle's task is on the fair!

Judging by the black exhaust residue on the side of the body, this Guy Big J4 has a generator inside the van body. According to the grille badge it is fitted with the 'showman's friend', the good old Gardner engine. It was seen at Retford in 1990.

J. T. Pearson of Derby parked this Staffordshire-registered Foden S20 eight-wheeler behind the old Checkley Café between fairs in 1985. It was actually there for a few weeks and hidden from view, but keen-eyed enthusiasts have a knack for seeking out such gems.

Yet another vehicle pressed into service, and still in the previous owner's livery, was this ex-Plasmor Foden Haulmaster eight-wheeler and trailer, which forms a funhouse when built up. This was spotted at Truck Haven, Carnforth, on 23 August 1994.

The author with the Warwick family's Foden Alpha tractor unit. The 'Cage Fighter' Meteorite ride that he operated is in the background. Quarry Park, Shrewsbury, 10 June 2017.

Acknowledgements

Being no expert, a book on fairground lorries is not the easiest subject to research due to some vehicles being 'anonymous' with no operator's names being apparent. It is not always easy to find out details, so I am in debt to the following people who have provided information on vehicles, locations and rides, etc.

My thanks go to the Warwick family from Stoke-on-Trent, with whom I have always held in high regard; Steve Smith of the Fairground Society, who is the most versed expert on fairs that I have ever met; and Chris Gardner and Nigel Addy, who have provided vital vehicle information. As an addition, in this day and age I must also mention the internet and social media, where there are several sites dedicated to the fairgrounds. More than once vital information has been provided by fellow enthusiasts on these sites. It is inevitable that even drawing on these sources, some vehicles have escaped the combined scrutiny, thus remaining anonymous. For this, again, my humble apologies.

I must also say that I am not a professional photographer; in fact, far from it! However, the need to record vehicles on film for posterity was always the aim, and pre-digital days it wasn't until the slides arrived back from the developers that the results could be viewed. Sometimes the results left little to be desired, but to replicate the scene was virtually impossible, so they are what they are. Some slides in my collection are now over forty years old, and, like me, have aged. I do hope the quality doesn't detract from the end result.